Reading Advantage

Student Journal

Laura Robb • James F. Baumann • Carol J. Fuhler • Joan Kindig

Avon Connell-Cowell • R. Craig Roney • Jo Worthy

GReaT SouRCe®
EDUCATION GROUP
A Division of Houghton Mifflin Company

International Standard Book Number-13: 978-0-669-50648-8
International Standard Book Number-10: 0-669-50648-6

1 2 3 4 5 6 7 8 9 10 - DBH - 12 11 10 09 08 07 06

ii

Contents

Money Magazine

Building Vocabulary: Knowledge Rating Chart

Show your knowledge of each word by adding information to the other boxes in the row.

Word	Define or Use in a Sentence	Where Have I Seen or Heard It?	How Is It Used in the Selection?	Looks Like (Words or Sketch)
bristled				
degrading				
stereotypes				
prominent				
hiatus				

Writing: Double-entry Journal

In the left-hand column, write quotations from the selection. Then, in the right-hand column, write your reaction to each quotation.

Quotations	My Thoughts

Building Vocabulary: Words with Multiple Meanings

What other words do you know that have more than one meaning?
Write the words and the definitions below. Two are listed for you.
Think of others or look for some in the selection.

Word	First Definition	Second Definition
bristled	to become angry or annoyed	bristle: short, stiff hair of a boar, used to make hairbrushes
tone		
hail		

Building Vocabulary: Predictions

How do you predict these words will be used in "Kids Behind the Camera"? Write your answers in the second column. Next, read the article. Then, clarify your answers in the third column.

Word	My prediction for how the word will be used	How the word is actually used
documentary		
Buddhist		
vacuum		
scripts		
exile		
tolerance		

Writing: Interview

Write your interview questions about another student's interests. Then read the questions to the student and write the responses. Make sure you ask follow-up questions that help the interviewee elaborate and extend the response.

Question:_____

_____

Response:_____

_____

_____

_____

Question:_____

_____

Response:_____

_____

_____

_____

Question:_____

_____

Response:_____

_____

_____

Building Vocabulary: Using Context to Understand a Word

Select a vocabulary word from the article that you defined from the context.
Complete the statements and answer the questions about your word.

My Word in Context:

I think this word means _____

because _____

_____

_____

My word is _____

_____

My word is not _____

_____

Where else might I find this word? _____

_____

_____

What makes this an important word to know? _____

_____

_____

_____

_____

Building Vocabulary: Synonyms Chart

Choose three other words from the selection. For each word, think of three synonyms (words similar in meaning). Use a thesaurus to help you, if you wish.

Vocabulary Word	Synonyms
haphazardly	1. disorderly 2. casually 3. randomly
	1. 2. 3.
	1. 2. 3.
	1. 2. 3.

Writing: Character Map

Use what you have learned about one character in
"Miss Understanding" to fill in the character map.

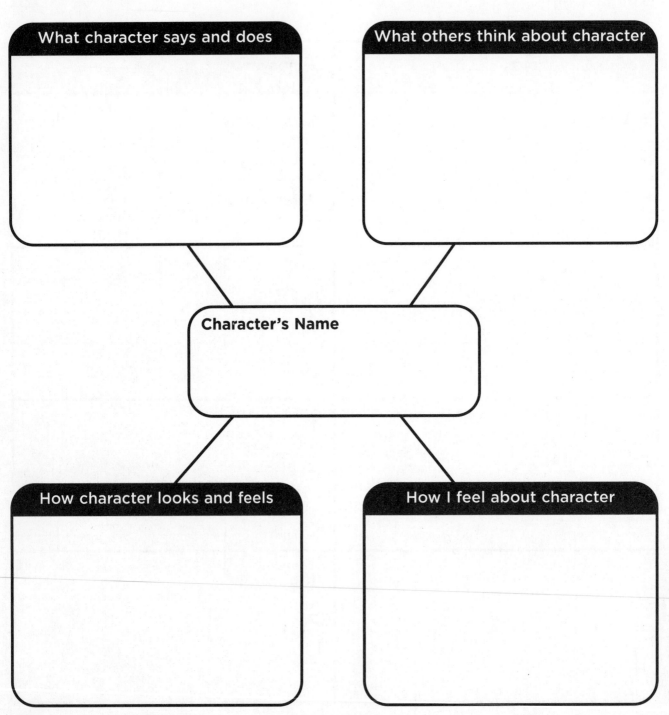

What character says and does

What others think about character

Character's Name

How character looks and feels

How I feel about character

Name _____ Date _____

Writing: Dialogue for a New Scene

Use the information from the previous page to write the next scene in "Miss Understanding." First, list the two characters you have chosen. Then, write the dialogue.

Characters: _____ **and** _____

As the scene opens, _____

_____

_____

_____

_____

_____

_____

_____

_____

_____

_____

_____

_____

_____

_____

_____

_____

_____

_____

_____

_____

Building Vocabulary: Denotation and Connotation

Choose three words from the selection. For each word, write a definition in the denotation box. Then, in the connotation box, write some personal associations you have with the word. Last, tell where you might see the word used.

Word	Denotation (general meaning)	Connotation (personal association)
deteriorating	growing worse	a building that is falling apart
	Where might I see this word? I might see this word in an article about an old house.	
1.		
	Where might I see this word?	
2.		
	Where might I see this word?	
3.		
	Where might I see this word?	

Building Vocabulary: Using a Word Map

Write a vocabulary word in the center box. Write a definition. Next, read the selection. Then, answer the questions to complete the map.

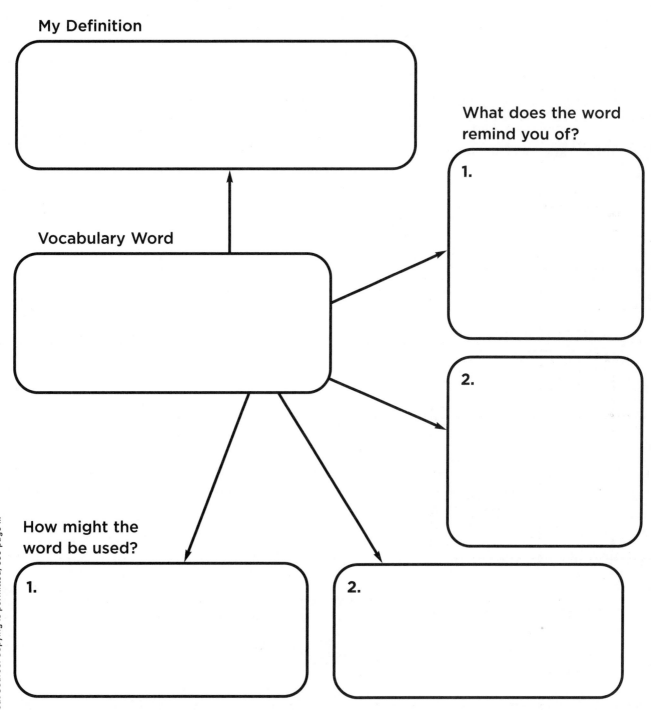

My Definition

What does the word remind you of?

1.

2.

Vocabulary Word

How might the word be used?

1.

2.

Writing: Letter to the Editor

Write a letter to the editor of your local paper about the need for new signs in your school. Draw the symbols for these signs in the boxes. Write the meanings of the symbols. Add your name to the end of the letter.

Dear Editor,

I strongly feel that we need some new signs to help visitors find their way around our school and locate the things they need. All these signs can give their messages with symbols, not words. Here are my suggestions.

Symbols   **Meanings**

_____

_____

_____

_____

_____

_____

_____

_____

_____

Yours truly,

Building Vocabulary: Related Words

Read each vocabulary word. Then write its base word. Think of another word that is related to the vocabulary word and its base word. Write the related word and its definition.

Vocabulary Word	Base Word	Related Word	Definition of Related Word
interpretations	interpret	interpreter	someone who interprets
modified			
controversies			
depicted			

Building Vocabulary: Concept Ladder

Answer the questions to complete the concept ladder.

Write words or phrases to record your responses.

Concept

What is it also called?

What is it used for?

Where is it common?

What is it made of?

What does it look like?

Writing: Travel Brochure

Write a two-page travel brochure about either the area in which you live or a special place in your state. Start on this page and continue on the next page. Write and sketch.

Writing: Travel Brochure

Continue your travel brochure on this page.

Communication • Guanajuato, Mexico

Building Vocabulary: Prefix *sub-*

Write words you know that contain the prefix *sub-*. Write a
definition for each word. Use a dictionary to help you, if you wish.

---

sub- means "under, to a lesser degree than, to lower in rank or importance"

Word	Definition
subterranean	underground

Building Vocabulary: Making Associations

Pick two words from the vocabulary list below. Think about what you already know about each word and answer the questions.

controversy	facilitated	safe house	mnemonic
fashion	oral history	internment	

Word _____

What do you think about when you read this word? _____

_____

Who might use this word? _____

_____

What do you already know about this word? _____

_____

Word _____

What do you think about when you read this word? _____

_____

Who might use this word? _____

_____

What do you already know about this word? _____

_____

Now watch for these words in the magazine selection. Were you on the right track?

Name _____ Date _____

Writing: Quilt Design

Create a quilt design based on something important in your life.
Then write to explain the message behind the quilt's design.

Quilt Design

Explanation: _____

_____

_____

_____

_____

_____

_____

_____

_____

_____

_____

_____

Building Vocabulary: Open Compound Words

Combine pairs of words from the box to make six more open compound words. Then write a definition for each. Use a dictionary for help, if you wish.

fire	opera	face	school
value	hot	board	extinguisher
dog	engine	glasses	mask

Open Compound Words	Meaning
hot dog	a sandwich made with a frankfurter enclosed in a split roll

Building Vocabulary: Predictions

How do you predict these words will be used in "Ren4, Communicator"? Write your answers in the second column. Next, read the story. Then, clarify your answers in the third column.

Word	My prediction for how the word will be used	How the word is actually used
tether		
lush		
components		
dialects		
vivid		
bizarre		
module		

Writing: Double-entry Journal

In the left-hand column, write quotations from the selection that tell something about Ren4's life or character. In the right-hand column, write inferences you make about him from each quotation.

Quotations	Inferences

Building Vocabulary: Synonyms

When choosing a synonym, it is important to choose the one closest in meaning to the word it is replacing.

Read the vocabulary words in the first column. In the third column, list three synonyms for each word. Refer to the page number and read the sentence in the selection that contains the vocabulary word. Decide which synonym could best replace the vocabulary word. Write the synonym in the fourth column.

Vocabulary Word	Found on page:	Synonyms	Best Synonym
vivid	38	1. clear 2. 3.	
bizarre	38	1. 2. 3.	
lush	35	1. 2. 3.	
components	35	1. 2. 3.	

Building Vocabulary: Knowledge Rating Chart

Show your knowledge of each word by adding information to the other boxes in the row.

Word	Define or Use in a Sentence	Where Have I Seen or Heard It?	How Is It Used in the Selection?	Looks Like (Words or Sketch)
sentinels				
infrasound				
larynx				
tsunami				
sophisticated				
replicate				
empathize				

Writing: 5Ws Chart

The 5Ws—*who, what, where, when,* and *why*—give readers the basic information about a nonfiction text. What do the 5Ws tell you about "Silent No More"?

5Ws	Details from "Silent No More"
Who is the article about?	
What happens?	
Where do the major events take place?	
When do the major events take place?	
Why are the events important?	

Writing: News Story

Use the 5Ws chart you completed on page 25 to write a short news story about Ms. Von Muggenthaler's findings about giraffes and infrasound communication.

_____

_____

_____

_____

_____

_____

_____

_____

_____

_____

_____

_____

_____

_____

_____

_____

Building Vocabulary: Creating a Word Web

Add details around the oval that help define the word. Then write the complete definition below.

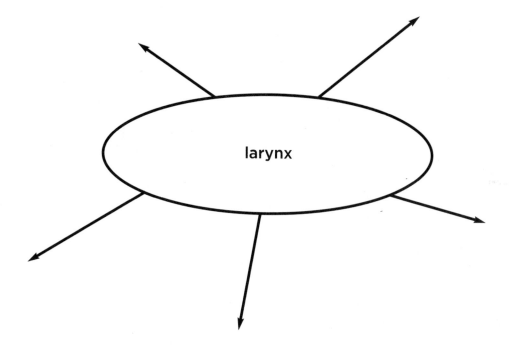

Write the complete definition here:

Building Vocabulary: Using a Word Map

Write a vocabulary word in the center box. Write a definition. Next, read the selection. Then, answer the questions to complete the map.

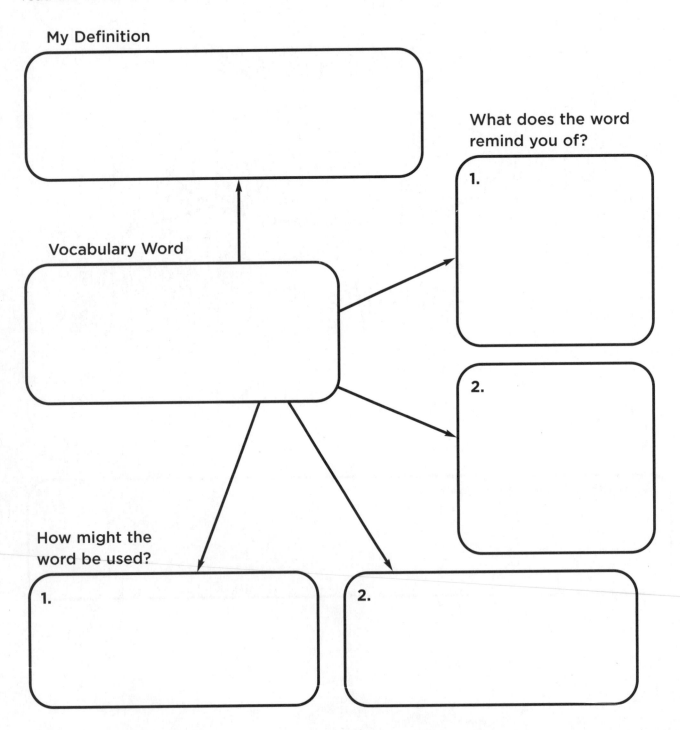

My Definition

Vocabulary Word

What does the word remind you of?

1.

2.

How might the word be used?

1.

2.

Reading Advantage

Student Journal

Laura Robb • James F. Baumann • Carol J. Fuhler • Joan Kindig

Avon Connell-Cowell • R. Craig Roney • Jo Worthy

GReaT SouRCe®
EDUCATION GROUP
A Division of Houghton Mifflin Company

International Standard Book Number-13: 978-0-669-50648-8
International Standard Book Number-10: 0-669-50648-6

1 2 3 4 5 6 7 8 9 10 - DBH - 12 11 10 09 08 07 06

Contents

Building Vocabulary: Knowledge Rating Chart

Show your knowledge of each word by adding information to the other boxes in the row.

Word	Define or Use in a Sentence	Where Have I Seen or Heard It?	How Is It Used in the Selection?	Looks Like (Words or Sketch)
bristled				
degrading				
stereotypes				
prominent				
hiatus				

Writing: Double-entry Journal

In the left-hand column, write quotations from the selection. Then, in the right-hand column, write your reaction to each quotation.

Quotations	My Thoughts

Building Vocabulary: Words with Multiple Meanings

What other words do you know that have more than one meaning?

Write the words and the definitions below. Two are listed for you.

Think of others or look for some in the selection.

Word	First Definition	Second Definition
bristled	to become angry or annoyed	bristle: short, stiff hair of a boar, used to make hairbrushes
tone		
hail		

Building Vocabulary: Predictions

How do you predict these words will be used in "Kids Behind the Camera"? Write your answers in the second column. Next, read the article. Then, clarify your answers in the third column.

Word	My prediction for how the word will be used	How the word is actually used
documentary		
Buddhist		
vacuum		
scripts		
exile		
tolerance		

Name _____ Date _____

Writing: Interview

Write your interview questions about another student's interests. Then read the questions to the student and write the responses. Make sure you ask follow-up questions that help the interviewee elaborate and extend the response.

Question:_____

_____

Response:_____

_____

_____

_____

Question:_____

_____

Response:_____

_____

_____

_____

Question:_____

_____

Response:_____

_____

_____

Building Vocabulary: Using Context to Understand a Word

Select a vocabulary word from the article that you defined from the context.
Complete the statements and answer the questions about your word.

> **My Word in Context:**

I think this word means _____

because _____

_____

_____

My word is _____

_____

My word is not _____

_____

Where else might I find this word? _____

_____

_____

What makes this an important word to know? _____

_____

_____

_____

Building Vocabulary: Synonyms Chart

Choose three other words from the selection. For each word, think of three synonyms (words similar in meaning). Use a thesaurus to help you, if you wish.

Vocabulary Word	Synonyms
haphazardly	1. disorderly 2. casually 3. randomly
	1. 2. 3.
	1. 2. 3.
	1. 2. 3.

Writing: Character Map

Use what you have learned about one character in "Miss Understanding" to fill in the character map.

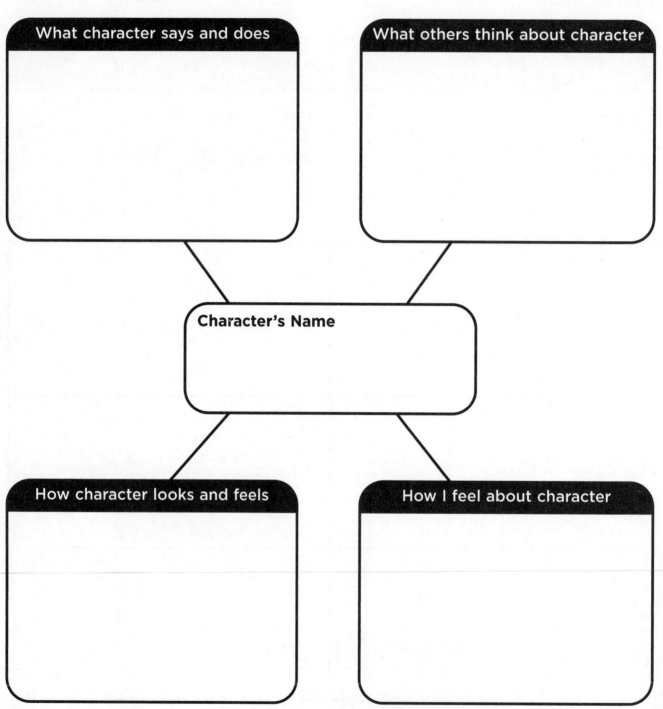

What character says and does

What others think about character

Character's Name

How character looks and feels

How I feel about character

Writing: Dialogue for a New Scene

Use the information from the previous page to write the next scene in "Miss Understanding." First, list the two characters you have chosen. Then, write the dialogue.

Characters: _____ **and** _____

As the scene opens, _____

_____

_____

_____

_____

_____

_____

_____

_____

_____

_____

_____

_____

_____

_____

_____

_____

_____

Building Vocabulary: Denotation and Connotation

Choose three words from the selection. For each word, write a definition in the denotation box. Then, in the connotation box, write some personal associations you have with the word. Last, tell where you might see the word used.

Word	Denotation (general meaning)	Connotation (personal association)
deteriorating	growing worse	a building that is falling apart
	Where might I see this word? I might see this word in an article about an old house.	
1.		
	Where might I see this word?	
2.		
	Where might I see this word?	
3.		
	Where might I see this word?	

Building Vocabulary: Using a Word Map

Write a vocabulary word in the center box. Write a definition. Next,
read the selection. Then, answer the questions to complete the map.

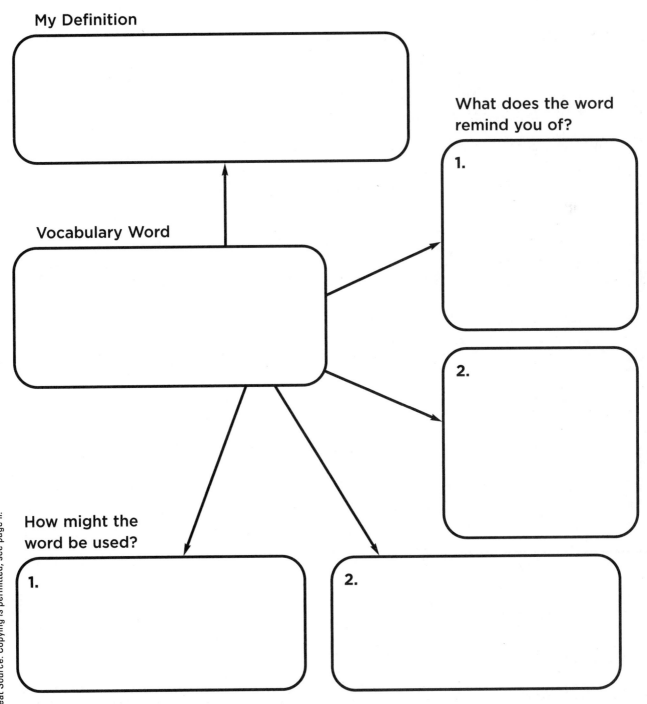

My Definition

**What does the word
remind you of?**

1.

Vocabulary Word

2.

**How might the
word be used?**

1.

2.

Writing: Letter to the Editor

Write a letter to the editor of your local paper about the need for new signs in your school. Draw the symbols for these signs in the boxes. Write the meanings of the symbols. Add your name to the end of the letter.

Dear Editor,

I strongly feel that we need some new signs to help visitors find their way around our school and locate the things they need. All these signs can give their messages with symbols, not words. Here are my suggestions.

Symbols	**Meanings**
	_____ _____ _____
	_____ _____ _____
	_____ _____ _____

Yours truly,

Building Vocabulary: Related Words

Read each vocabulary word. Then write its base word. Think of another word that is related to the vocabulary word and its base word. Write the related word and its definition.

Vocabulary Word	Base Word	Related Word	Definition of Related Word
interpretations	interpret	interpreter	someone who interprets
modified			
controversies			
depicted			

Building Vocabulary: Concept Ladder

Answer the questions to complete the concept ladder.
Write words or phrases to record your responses.

Concept

What is it also called?

What is it used for?

Where is it common?

What is it made of?

What does it look like?

Communication • Guanajuato, Mexico

Writing: Travel Brochure

Write a two-page travel brochure about either the area in which you live or a special place in your state. Start on this page and continue on the next page. Write and sketch.

Writing: Travel Brochure

Continue your travel brochure on this page.

Building Vocabulary: Prefix *sub-*

Write words you know that contain the prefix *sub-*. Write a definition for each word. Use a dictionary to help you, if you wish.

---

sub- means "under, to a lesser degree than, to lower in rank or importance"

Word	Definition
subterranean	underground

Building Vocabulary: Making Associations

Pick two words from the vocabulary list below. Think about what you already know about each word and answer the questions.

controversy	facilitated	safe house	mnemonic
fashion	oral history	internment	

Word_____

What do you think about when you read this word? _____

_____

Who might use this word? _____

_____

What do you already know about this word? _____

_____

Word_____

What do you think about when you read this word? _____

_____

Who might use this word? _____

_____

What do you already know about this word? _____

_____

Now watch for these words in the magazine selection. Were you on the right track?

Writing: Quilt Design

Create a quilt design based on something important in your life.
Then write to explain the message behind the quilt's design.

Quilt Design

Explanation: _____

_____

_____

_____

_____

_____

_____

_____

_____

_____

Building Vocabulary: Open Compound Words

Combine pairs of words from the box to make six more open compound words. Then write a definition for each. Use a dictionary for help, if you wish.

fire	opera	face	school
value	hot	board	extinguisher
dog	engine	glasses	mask

Open Compound Words	Meaning
hot dog	a sandwich made with a frankfurter enclosed in a split roll

Building Vocabulary: Predictions

How do you predict these words will be used in "Ren4, Communicator"? Write your answers in the second column. Next, read the story. Then, clarify your answers in the third column.

Word	My prediction for how the word will be used	How the word is actually used
tether		
lush		
components		
dialects		
vivid		
bizarre		
module		

Writing: Double-entry Journal

In the left-hand column, write quotations from the selection that tell something about Ren4's life or character. In the right-hand column, write inferences you make about him from each quotation.

Quotations	Inferences

Building Vocabulary: Synonyms

When choosing a synonym, it is important to choose the one closest in meaning to the word it is replacing.

Read the vocabulary words in the first column. In the third column, list three synonyms for each word. Refer to the page number and read the sentence in the selection that contains the vocabulary word. Decide which synonym could best replace the vocabulary word. Write the synonym in the fourth column.

Vocabulary Word	Found on page:	Synonyms	Best Synonym
vivid	38	1. clear 2. 3.	
bizarre	38	1. 2. 3.	
lush	35	1. 2. 3.	
components	35	1. 2. 3.	

Building Vocabulary: Knowledge Rating Chart

Show your knowledge of each word by adding information to the other boxes in the row.

Word	Define or Use in a Sentence	Where Have I Seen or Heard It?	How Is It Used in the Selection?	Looks Like (Words or Sketch)
sentinels				
infrasound				
larynx				
tsunami				
sophisticated				
replicate				
empathize				

Writing: 5Ws Chart

The 5Ws—*who, what, where, when,* and *why*—give readers the basic information about a nonfiction text. What do the 5Ws tell you about "Silent No More"?

5Ws	Details from "Silent No More"
Who is the article about?	
What happens?	
Where do the major events take place?	
When do the major events take place?	
Why are the events important?	

Writing: News Story

Use the 5Ws chart you completed on page 25 to write a short news story about Ms. Von Muggenthaler's findings about giraffes and infrasound communication.

_____

_____

_____

_____

_____

_____

_____

_____

_____

_____

_____

_____

_____

_____

_____

_____

_____

Building Vocabulary: Creating a Word Web

Add details around the oval that help define the word. Then write the complete definition below.

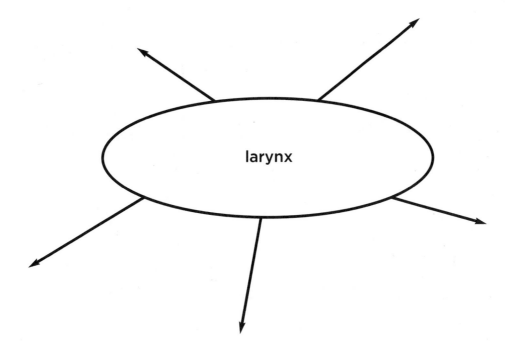

larynx

Write the complete definition here:

Building Vocabulary: Using a Word Map

Write a vocabulary word in the center box. Write a definition. Next, read the selection. Then, answer the questions to complete the map.

My Definition

Vocabulary Word

What does the word remind you of?

1.

2.

How might the word be used?

1.

2.

Name .... Date ....

Writing: Story String

Complete the story string to retell what happened in "I Am Not
Wanda Wigglesworth."

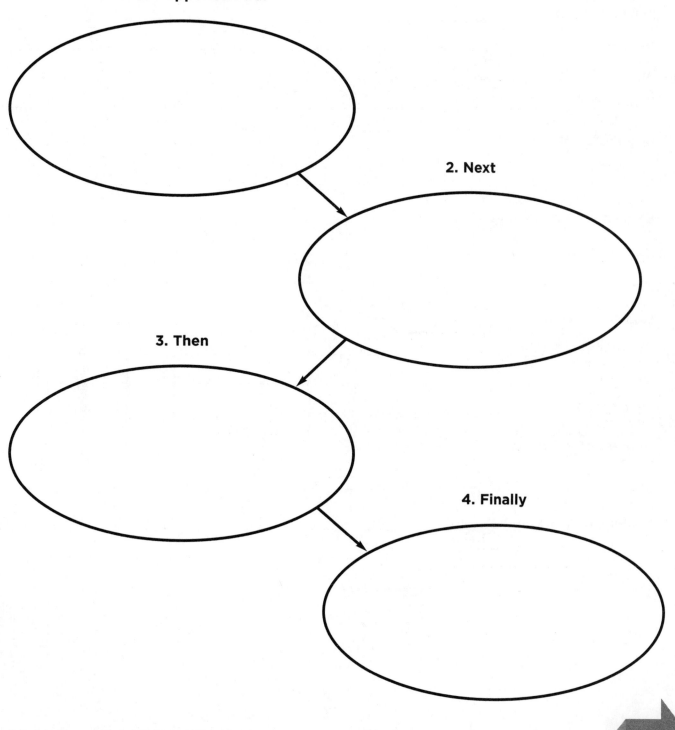

1. What Happened First

2. Next

3. Then

4. Finally

Building Vocabulary: Degrees of Meaning

Some words that are synonyms have stronger meanings than others.
Choose two words from the selection. Write three synonyms for each
word. Then rank the synonyms from weakest to strongest.

Selection Word: _____

Synonym 1: _____

Synonym 2: _____

Synonym 3: _____

Degrees of Meaning:

_____ ⟶ _____ ⟶ _____

Explain your reasoning: _____

_____

_____

Selection Word: _____

Synonym 1: _____

Synonym 2: _____

Synonym 3: _____

Degrees of Meaning:

_____ ⟶ _____ ⟶ _____

Explain your reasoning: _____

_____

_____

Building Vocabulary: Concept Ladder

Use the vocabulary word *civilians* to answer the questions and complete the concept ladder. Your responses may be in the form of words, phrases, or sentences.

Concept

Who are they?

Where have you heard about them?

What ideas do you associate with them?

What is an example of how they might be written or spoken about?

Writing: Biographical Sketch

Using the information in the selection, write a biographical sketch of
Peter Dut. Refer to the notes you took.

_____

_____

_____

_____

_____

_____

_____

_____

_____

_____

_____

_____

_____

_____

_____

_____

_____

_____

_____

_____

_____

_____

_____

_____

_____

Building Vocabulary: Related Words

Read each word. Then write its base word. Think of another word that is related to the word and the base word. Write the related word and its definition. You may use a dictionary to help you, if you wish.

Vocabulary Word	Base Word	Related Word	Definition of Related Word
civilians	civil	civilization	high level of progress
documentary			
government			
political			

Building Vocabulary: Making Associations

Pick two words from the vocabulary list below. Think about what you already know about each word and answer the questions.

encroaching	domain	sprawl	dwindling
predators	menacing	confrontations	

Word _____

What do you think about when you read this word? _____

_____

Who might use this word? _____

_____

What do you already know about this word? _____

_____

Word _____

What do you think about when you read this word? _____

_____

Who might use this word? _____

_____

What do you already know about this word? _____

_____

Now watch for these words in the magazine selection. Were you on the right track?

Writing: Notes for Visualizing

Which part of the article could you visualize best? Describe it below.
Include as many details as you can. Then draw a picture of how you
imagined it in your mind.

The part of the article I could visualize best was _____

_____

_____

Some details I "saw in my mind" include _____

_____

_____

_____

Now draw what you visualized.

Building Vocabulary: Using Context to Understand a Word

Select a vocabulary word or another word from the selection that you
defined from the context. Complete the statements and answer the
questions about your word.

My Word in Context:

I think this word means _____

_____

because _____

_____

My word is _____

_____

My word is not _____

_____

Where else might I find this word?_____

_____

_____

What makes this an important word to know?_____

_____

_____

_____

_____

Building Vocabulary: Predictions

How do you predict these words will be used in "Sweet Company"?
Write your answers in the second column. Next, read the selection.
Then, clarify your answers in the third column.

Word	My prediction for how the word will be used	How the word is actually used
pollinate		
nectar		
pollen		
larva		
debris		
barbs		

Writing: Illustrated Glossary

Create an illustrated glossary. Choose six terms from the text and write a definition for each word. In the third column, draw an illustration that will help people understand the word's meaning.

Term	Definition	Illustration
1. _____		
2. _____		
3. _____		
4. _____		
5. _____		
6. _____		

Building Vocabulary: Denotation and Connotation

Choose three vocabulary words. For each word, write a definition in the denotation box. Then, in the connotation box, write the personal associations the word has for you. Last, tell where you might see the word used. The word *pollen* has been done as an example.

---

pollinate   nectar   larva   debris   barbs

Word	Denotation (general meaning)	Connotation (personal association)
pollen	microspores that are released from flowers to fertilize other flowers	causes allergic reactions, such as watery eyes and constant sneezing
	Where might I see this word? Weather reports have something called the "pollen count."	
1.		
	Where might I see this word?	
2.		
	Where might I see this word?	
3.		
	Where might I see this word?	

Building Vocabulary: Knowledge Rating Chart

Show your knowledge of each word by adding information to the other boxes in the row.

Word	Define or Use in a Sentence	Where Have I Seen or Heard It?	How Is It Used in the Selection?	Looks Like (Words or Sketch)
reservoir				
surveyed				
merchandise				
indentured servant				
aqueducts				
displaced				

Writing: Plan for Play Scene

Use ideas from the class discussion and the information in the epilogue on page 56 to write the next scene in "The Lost Towns of the Catskill Mountains." First, list three characters whom you would like to appear in your scene, with a brief description of each. Then, make notes about ideas you will include in the scene.

My Cast of Characters

Name	Description

Notes for Scene

_____

_____

_____

_____

_____

_____

_____

_____

_____

Writing: Play Scene

Write the play scene you planned. Use as many lines as you need for
each character's dialogue.

Character   **Dialogue**

_____

_____

_____

_____

_____

_____

_____

_____

_____

_____

_____

_____

_____

_____

_____

_____

_____

_____

_____

Building Vocabulary: Parts of Speech Word Sort

How are each of the words below used by Otis Fields on page 55 of "The Lost Towns of the Catskill Mountains"? Sort each word according to its use into the proper category below.

Noun: Naming word

Verb: Action word

Adjective: Describing word

name	Fields	offering	answer
needs	living	drinking	country

Noun			Verb	Adjective
Person	**Place**	**Thing**		

Building Vocabulary: Making Associations

Pick two words from the vocabulary list below. Think about what you already know about each word and answer the questions.

espionage	internment	internees

Word _____

What do you think about when you read this word? _____

_____

Who might use this word? _____

_____

What do you already know about this word? _____

_____

Word _____

What do you think about when you read this word? _____

_____

Who might use this word? _____

_____

What do you already know about this word? _____

_____

Now watch for these words in the magazine article. Were you on the right track?

Writing: Double-entry Journal

In the first column, write phrases or sentences from "They're Sending Us Away!" that were especially interesting or meaningful to you. In the second column, explain the significance of each quotation.

Quotation	Why It Is Meaningful

Name _____ Date _____

Building Vocabulary: Creating a Word Web

In the center oval, write a vocabulary word or another word from the selection. Add details around the oval that help define the word. Then write the complete definition below.

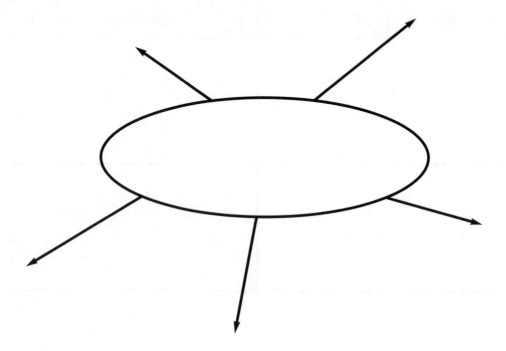

Write the complete definition here:

Relationships • They're Sending Us Away! *and* Three Wishes

Building Vocabulary: Making Associations

Pick two words from the vocabulary list below. Think about what you already know about each word and answer the questions.

---

dilemmas   congestion   mimic   propel

Word _____

What do you think about when you read this word? _____

_____

Who might use this word? _____

_____

What do you already know about this word? _____

_____

Word _____

What do you think about when you read this word? _____

_____

Who might use this word? _____

_____

What do you already know about this word? _____

_____

Now watch for these words in the magazine article. Were you on the right track?

Writing: Planning Chart

Use this chart to help you plan a summary of "Cutting Edge Cool."
Go back through the selection and take notes on both the inventions
themselves and the author's main ideas about inventors and inventions.

Invention	Brief Description	Purpose

Main ideas about inventors and inventions:

Writing: Summary

Refer to the planning chart you completed on page 80 and write a summary of "Cutting Edge Cool." Remember to include some main ideas from the selection, as well as information on the different inventions.

_____

_____

_____

_____

_____

_____

_____

_____

_____

_____

_____

_____

_____

_____

_____

_____

_____

_____

_____

_____

_____

_____

Building Vocabulary: Illustrated Mini-Dictionary

Create an illustrated mini-dictionary. For each vocabulary word,
write a definition on the lines. Then draw a picture below that
shows the word's meaning. You may use a dictionary, if you wish.

dilemmas _____

_____

_____

_____

congestion _____

_____

_____

_____

mimic _____

_____

_____

_____

propel _____

_____

_____

_____

Name _____ Date _____

Building Vocabulary: Creating an Illustrated Word Web

Choose a vocabulary word and write it in the center oval. Add details and/or pictures around the oval that help define the word. Then write the complete definition below.

reef	protruded	scuba	sediment
salvage	artifacts	hull	

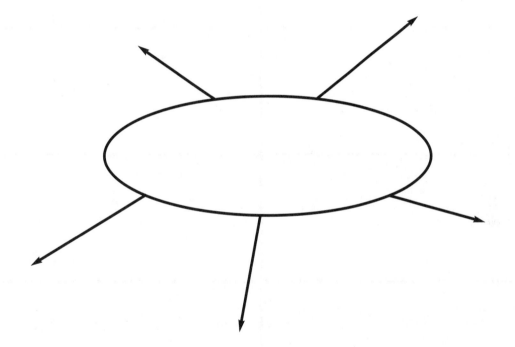

Write the complete definition here:

Writing: Double-entry Journal

In the left-hand column, write quotations from the selection. Then,
in the right-hand column, write your reaction to each quotation.

Quotation	Why It Is Meaningful

Name_____ Date_____

Building Vocabulary: Using Context to Understand a Word

Select a vocabulary word you defined from the context. Complete
the statements and answer the questions about your word.

---

reef   protruded   scuba   sediment   salvage   artifacts   hull

---

My Word in Context:

I think this word means _____

because _____

_____

_____

My word is _____

_____

My word is not _____

_____

Where else might I find this word?_____

_____

_____

What makes this an important word to know?_____

_____

_____

_____

Building Vocabulary: Knowledge Rating Chart

Show your knowledge of each word by adding information to the other boxes in the row.

Word	Define or Use in a Sentence	Where Have I Seen or Heard It?	How Is It Used in the Selection?	Looks Like (Words or Sketch)
alterations				
commission				
reposition				
drastically				
characteristics				
reputation				

Writing: Announcement

Write an announcement asking for an artist to create a commissioned work for you. Remember to include a catchy headline, or lead; a description of the item; the goal of the commission; the way you'd like the artists to respond; and your contact information. Refer to the plan you made.

_____

_____

_____

_____

_____

_____

_____

_____

_____

_____

_____

_____

_____

_____

_____

_____

_____

_____

_____

_____

_____

_____

Building Vocabulary: Prefix *re-*

There are many words in the selection that have the prefix *re-*, such as *reposition*. Can you find four more? Write each word in the first column and its definition in the second column.

re- means "to do again"

Word	Definition
reposition	to put in a different place

Discoveries • Not Just Horsing Around

Building Vocabulary: Using a Word Map

Write a vocabulary word in the center box. Next, read the selection.
Write a definition. Then, answer the questions to complete the map.

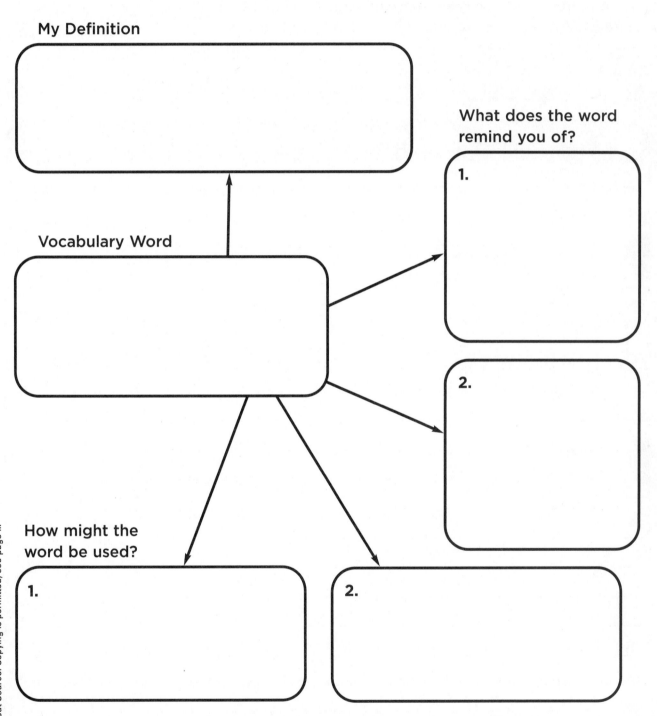

My Definition

Vocabulary Word

What does the word remind you of?

1.

2.

How might the word be used?

1.

2.

Writing: Alien Journal Entries

Imagine that you are an alien visiting Earth for the first time. On this page and on page 91, write two journal entries documenting your journey to Earth and your contact with earthlings. Refer to the ideas you jotted down in your chart.

DATE _____

My Journey to Earth

_____

_____

_____

_____

_____

_____

_____

_____

_____

_____

_____

_____

_____

_____

_____

Name _____ Date _____

Writing: Alien Journal Entries

You are an alien visiting Earth for the first time. Write your second journal entry documenting your contact with earthlings. Refer to the ideas you jotted down in your chart.

DATE _____

My Contact with Earthlings

_____

_____

_____

_____

_____

_____

_____

_____

_____

_____

_____

_____

_____

_____

_____

_____

_____

Building Vocabulary: Combining Form *astro-*

In the first column, write four more words that begin with the combining form *astro-*. In the second column, write the definition of each word. Use a dictionary for help.

---

astro- means "star or other heavenly body"

Word	Definition
astronaut	pilot or member of a crew that goes into space

Discoveries • Is There Anybody Out There?

Building Vocabulary: Making Associations

Pick three words from the vocabulary list below. Think about what you already know about each word and answer the questions.

---

manual   permits   alternative   disability   infinitely

Word _____

What do you think about when you read this word? _____

Who might use this word? _____

What do you already know about this word? _____

_____

Word _____

What do you think about when you read this word? _____

Who might use this word? _____

What do you already know about this word? _____

_____

Word _____

What do you think about when you read this word? _____

Who might use this word? _____

What do you already know about this word? _____

_____

Now watch for these words in the magazine selection. Were you on the right track?

Writing: Somebody Wanted But So

Use this chart to help you organize your thoughts for a summary of "Taking the Right Turn."

	My Notes
Somebody (an important character)	
Wanted (a key problem with details)	
But (conflict for the character)	
So (an outcome)	

Now write your summary.

_____

_____

_____

_____

_____

_____

_____

_____

_____

_____

_____

Name_____ Date_____

Building Vocabulary: Words with Multiple Meanings

Find three more multiple-meaning words in the selection. Write each
word in the first column and its definitions in the second and third
columns. Use a dictionary to help you, if necessary.

Word	First Definition	Second Definition
permits	documents giving permission to do something	allows; gives consent to

Building Vocabulary: Concept Ladder

Use the vocabulary word *tsunamis* to answer the questions to complete the concept ladder. Write words, phrases, or sentences to record your responses. You may use a dictionary and a thesaurus to help you.

Concept

tsunamis

What is it?

Where is it found?

What causes it?

What are other words for it?

Name_____ Date_____

Writing: Cause/Effect Organizer

Write what might happen as a result of carrying out the spacecraft plan and the missile plan for deflecting an asteroid from Earth.

Spacecraft Plan	**Missile Plan**
Action (Cause)	**Action (Cause)**

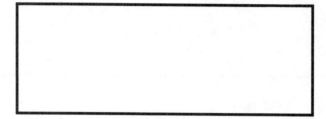

Result (Effect)

Result (Effect)
(New Cause)

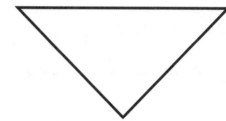

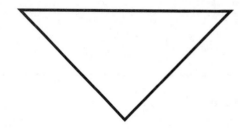

Result (Effect)

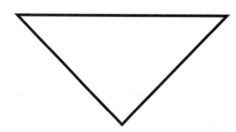

Building Vocabulary: Antonym Chart

All the words in the chart are in the selection. Find an antonym
for each word. Use a thesaurus and a dictionary to help you.

Word	Antonym
suddenly	gradually
destroy	
extinct	
plunge	
result	
fictional	

Building Vocabulary: Knowledge Rating Chart

Show your knowledge of each word by adding information to the other boxes in the row.

Word	Define or Use in a Sentence	Where Have I Seen or Heard It?	How Is It Used in the Selection?	Looks Like (Words or Sketch)
paleontologist				
ossified				
pertain				
crinoid				
invertebrates				
continuity				
stipend				

Writing: Personal Journal

Write a journal entry to tell about what you experience and learn in your classes on a given day. Don't forget to date your entry.

Name _____ Date _____

Building Vocabulary: Suffixes *-ology* and *-ologist*

Write words that you know that have these suffixes. Then write the definition of each word, using the information in the box.

-logy means "the study of _____"   **-ologist** means "a scientist who studies _____"

Word	Definition
geology	the study of the earth
geologist	a scientist who studies the earth

Name .... Date ....

Building Vocabulary: Predictions

How do you predict these words will be used in "Nanotechnology"?
Write your answers in the second column. Next, read the selection.
Then, clarify your answers in the third column.

Word	My prediction for how the word will be used	How the word is actually used
nanoscience		
atoms		
molecules		
antimicrobial		

Writing: Main Idea and Details Chart

First, write details from the section called "No More Scrubbing."

Then, use the details to help you figure out the main idea.

Main Idea:

Detail:	**Detail:**	**Detail:**

Writing: Summary

Use the information in the main idea and details chart on page 103 to write a one-paragraph summary of the section called "No More Scrubbing." Use your main idea to start or to end the paragraph.

Name _____ Date _____

Building Vocabulary: Using Context to Understand a Word

Select a vocabulary word or other word from the selection that you
defined from the context. Complete the statements and answer the
questions about your word.

My Word in Context:

I think this word means _____

because _____

_____

_____

My word is _____

_____

My word is not _____

_____

Where else might I find this word? _____

_____

_____

What makes this an important word to know? _____

_____

_____

_____

_____

Building Vocabulary: Making Associations

Pick two words from the vocabulary list below. Think about what you already know about each word and answer the questions.

---

patent   prototypes   inducted   sign language

Word _____

What do you think about when you read this word? _____

_____

Who might use this word? _____

_____

What do you already know about this word? _____

_____

Word _____

What do you think about when you read this word? _____

_____

Who might use this word? _____

_____

What do you already know about this word? _____

_____

Now watch for these words in the magazine article. Were you on the right track?

Writing: Problem and Solution

Choose three inventions that were described in the selection. Identify the problem each inventor saw. Then identify the solution that he or she came up with.

Problem:	→	Solution:

Problem:	→	Solution:

Problem:	→	Solution:

Building Vocabulary: Definition by Examples

Write five examples in each column to show the meaning of each
word. Try to provide a variety of types of trademarks and copyrights.

Trademarks ™	Copyrights ©

Building Vocabulary: Using a Word Map

Write a vocabulary word in the center box. Write a definition.
Next, read the selection. Then, answer the questions to complete the map.

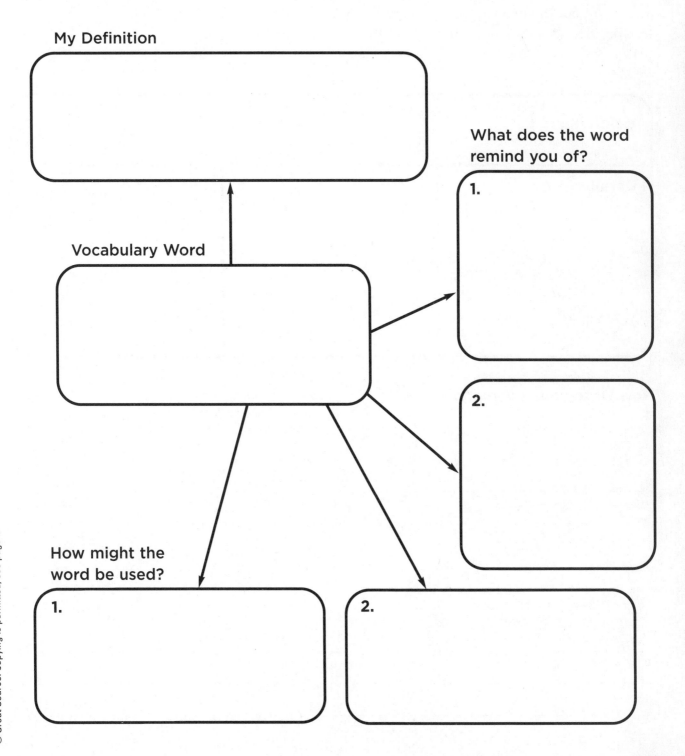

My Definition

Vocabulary Word

What does the word remind you of?

1.

2.

How might the word be used?

1.

2.

Writing: Main Idea and Details

First, write the details from the portion of the selection titled "An Investigator's Toolbox" (pages 51–52). Then, use the details to help you figure out the main idea. Finally, use the information in the chart to write a brief summary of that part of the article. Remember to use your main idea to start or to end the summary.

Main Idea:

Detail:	**Detail:**	**Detail:**

Now write your summary.

_____

_____

_____

_____

_____

_____

_____

_____

Building Vocabulary: Denotation and Connotation

Choose three vocabulary words. For each word, write a definition in the denotation box. Then, in the connotation box, write some personal associations you have with the word. Last, tell where you might see the word used.

| forensic | perpetrator | larvae |
| impressions | adhesive | latent |

Word	Denotation (general meaning)	Connotation (personal association)
1.		
	Where might I see this word?	
2.		
	Where might I see this word?	
3.		
	Where might I see this word?	

Building Vocabulary: Predictions

How do you predict these words or phrases will be used in "The Return of the Hound"? Write your answers in the second column. Next, read the play. Then, clarify your answers in the third column.

Word	My prediction for how the word will be used	How the word is actually used
luminous		
moor		
deduction		
infrared light		
superstition		

Writing: Chart and Summary

Use this chart to help you organize your thoughts for a summary of
the play "The Return of the Hound."

	My Notes
Somebody (an important character)	
Wanted (a key problem with details)	
But (conflict for the character)	
So (an outcome)	

Now write your summary.

_____

_____

_____

_____

_____

_____

_____

_____

_____

_____

_____

_____

_____

Building Vocabulary: Suffix *-ous*

Use what you know about the meaning of the base word plus the meaning of the suffix *-ous* to define each word.

-ous means "having," "full of," or "characterized by"

Word	Base Word	Definition
dangerous		
mysterious		
enormous		
murderous		
famous		
superstitious		

Building Vocabulary: Making Associations

Pick two words from the vocabulary list below. Think about what you already know about each word and answer the questions.

| anthropologist | archaeologists | hominids |
| genus | species | pygmy |

Word _____

What do you think about when you read this word? _____

_____

Who might use this word? _____

_____

What do you already know about this word? _____

_____

Word _____

What do you think about when you read this word? _____

_____

Who might use this word? _____

_____

What do you already know about this word? _____

_____

Now watch for these words in the magazine article. Were you on the right track?

Discoveries • Little People of the Island of Flores *and* Eureka!

115

Writing: Double-entry Journal

In the first column, write phrases or sentences from "Little People of the Island of Flores" that were especially interesting or meaningful to you in some way. In the second column, explain the significance of each quotation.

Quotation	Why It Is Meaningful

Building Vocabulary: Using Context to Understand a Word

Select a vocabulary word or other word from the selection that you defined from the context. Complete the statements and answer the questions about your word.

My Word in Context:

I think this word means _____

because _____

_____

_____

My word is _____

_____

My word is not _____

_____

Where else might I find this word? _____

_____

_____

What makes this an important word to know? _____

_____

_____

_____

_____

Building Vocabulary: Predictions

How do you predict these words will be used in "Taking Care of Business"? Write your answers in the second column. Next, read the selection. Then, clarify your answers in the third column.

Word	My prediction for how the word will be used	How the word is actually used
velocity		
impact		
promotion		
entrepreneurs		
statistics		
guarantees		

Writing: 5Ws Chart

Plan a short news story about one of the entrepreneurs in the selection "Taking Care of Business." Complete the 5Ws chart below by answering *who*, *what*, *where*, *when*, and *why* questions about the entrepreneur and his or her company.

5Ws	Details from "Taking Care of Business"
Who is the entrepreneur?	
What does the entrepreneur do?	
Where does he or she do it?	
When does (did) he or she do it?	
Why is this important or interesting?	

Writing: News Story

Use the 5Ws chart you completed on page 119 to write a short news story about one of the entrepreneurs in "Taking Care of Business." Create a catchy headline that will grab your readers' attention.

_____

_____

_____

_____

_____

_____

_____

_____

_____

_____

_____

_____

_____

_____

_____

_____

_____

Building Vocabulary: Prefix *pro-*

Write words you know that contain the prefix *pro-* meaning "in support of" or "moving forward." Then write a definition for each word. Use a dictionary to help you, if you wish.

---

pro- can mean "in support of" or "moving forward"

Word	Definition
promotion	doing things to support or move a cause forward

Building Vocabulary: Using a Word Map

Write a vocabulary word in the center box. Write a definition. Next, read the selection. Then, answer the questions to complete the map.

minted   cumbersome   commemorated   composition

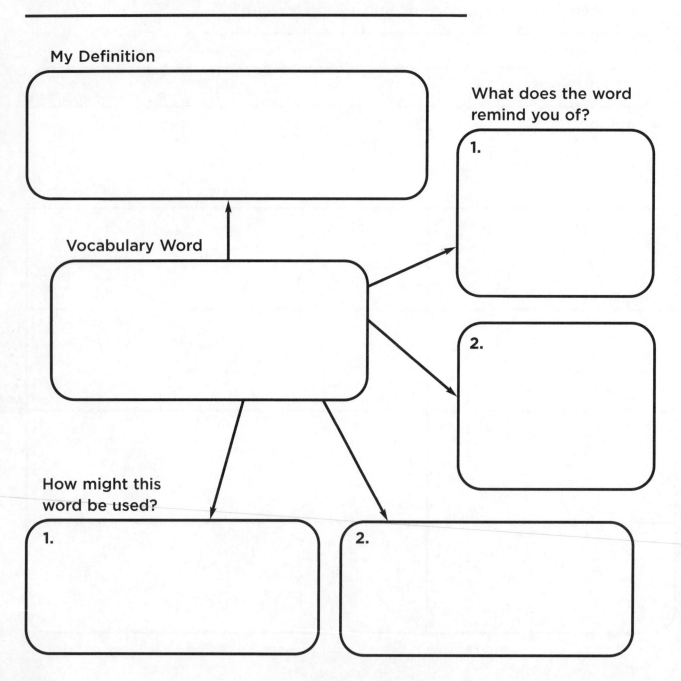

My Definition

Vocabulary Word

What does the word remind you of?

1.

2.

How might this word be used?

1.

2.

Writing: Pros/Cons Chart

With a partner, write lists of the pros (positive aspects) and cons (negative aspects) of keeping pennies in circulation.

Should We Keep the Penny?

Pros	Cons

Writing: Editorial

Use the information on one side of the pros/cons chart you created on page 123 to write an editorial expressing your opinion on whether we should keep the penny in circulation in the United States.

_____

_____

_____

_____

_____

_____

_____

_____

_____

_____

_____

_____

_____

_____

_____

_____

_____

_____

Building Vocabulary: Words with Multiple Meanings

What other words do you know that have more than one meaning?
Skim the selection "Penny Wise" for ideas. Write the words and two
definitions for each in the chart. One example is given.

Word	First Definition	Second Definition
mint	to produce coins	a candy-like item

Vocabulary Building: Knowledge Rating Chart

Show your knowledge of each word by adding information to the other boxes in the row.

Word	Define or Use in a Sentence	Where Have I Seen or Heard It?	How Is It Used in the Selection?	Looks Like (Words or Sketch)
implement				
charitable				
altruistic				
philanthropies				
under-utilized				
ruckus				

Writing: Double-entry Journal

In the first column, write phrases or sentences from "Generation
FIX-IT" that were especially interesting or meaningful to you in some
way. In the second column, explain the significance of each quotation.

Quotation	Why It Is Meaningful

Building Vocabulary: Suffix *-able*

In the first column, write words you know that are made up of a root word with the suffix *-able* added to it. Then write the root word. Write the definition of the word in the fourth column. Use a dictionary to help you, if you wish. One example is given.

-able means "able to, or having the ability to"

Word	Root Word	Suffix	Definition
charitable	charity	+ *-able*	able to be generous in giving to people who need help
		+ *-able*	
		+ *-able*	
		+ *-able*	

Building Vocabulary: Predictions

How do you predict these words will be used in "King Midas Redux"?
Write your answers in the second column. Next, read the play. Then,
clarify your answers in the third column.

Word	My prediction for how the word will be used	How the word is actually used
satyr		
oblivious		
dock		
cask		
obsequious		

Writing: Somebody Wanted But So Chart

Fill in this chart to help you organize your thoughts for a summary of the play "King Midas Redux." Then use the completed chart to write a summary of the play on page 131.

	My Notes
Somebody (an important character)	
Wanted (a key problem with details)	
But (conflict for the character)	
So (an outcome)	

Name _____ Date _____

Writing: Summary

Use your Somebody Wanted But So chart on page 130 to write a summary of the play "King Midas Redux."

_____

_____

_____

_____

_____

_____

_____

_____

_____

_____

_____

_____

_____

_____

_____

_____

_____

_____

_____

_____

_____

Building Vocabulary: Using Context to Understand a Word

Select a vocabulary word or other word from the selection that you defined from the context. Complete the statements and answer the questions about your word.

My Word in Context:

I think this word means _____

because _____

_____

_____

My word is _____

_____

My word is not _____

_____

Where else might I find this word? _____

_____

_____

What makes this an important word to know? _____

_____

_____

_____

_____

Building Vocabulary: Making Associations

Think about what you already know about each of the vocabulary words below and answer the questions.

Word _____ **occupation** _____

What do you think about when you read this word? _____

_____

Who might use this word? _____

What do you already know about this word? _____

_____

Word _____ **shortchange** _____

What do you think about when you read this word? _____

_____

Who might use this word? _____

What do you already know about this word? _____

_____

Word _____ **exclusion** _____

What do you think about when you read this word? _____

_____

Who might use this word? _____

What do you already know about this word? _____

_____

Now watch for these words in the magazine selection. Were you on the right track?

Writing: Interview

With a partner, choose a career described in "Making It Work."
Then write three interview questions you would like to ask someone
in that career. Role-play an interview with your partner and write his
or her responses.

Career: _____

Question: _____

_____

Response: _____

_____

_____

Question: _____

_____

Response: _____

_____

_____

Question: _____

_____

Response: _____

_____

_____

_____

Building Vocabulary: Creating a Word Web

Write details from the selection or your own experience that help to define or describe the word *occupation.* Then write the complete definition of the word in the box below. Use a dictionary to help you, if necessary.

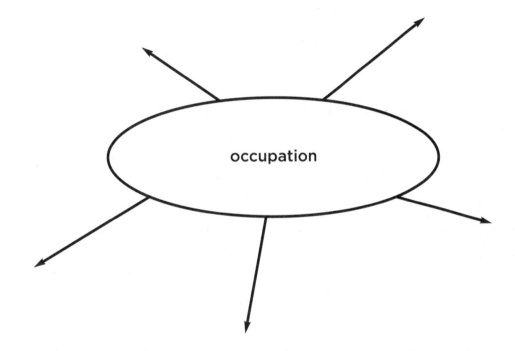

Write the complete definition here:

Building Vocabulary: Predictions

How do you predict these words or phrases will be used in "The Great Depression"? Write your answers in the second column. Next, read the selection. Then, clarify your answers in the third column.

Word	My prediction for how the word will be used	How the word is actually used
decimated		
devastating		
migrant labor		
fulfill		
foreclosed		

Writing: Notes for Visualizing

Which part of the selection could you visualize best? Describe it below. Then draw a picture of how you imagined it in your mind.

The part I could visualize best was _____

_____

_____

Some details I "saw in my mind" were _____

_____

_____

_____

Now draw what you visualized.

Building Vocabulary: Denotation and Connotation

Choose two vocabulary words. For each word, write a dictionary definition in the denotation box. Then, in the connotation box, write some personal associations you have with the word. Last, tell where you might see the word used.

| abominable | migrant labor | foreclosed |
| decimated | fulfill | |

Word	Denotation (general meaning)	Connotation (personal association)
devastating	very destructive	death of a family member
	Where might I see this word? news reports, autobiographies	
1.		
	Where might I see this word?	
2.		
	Where might I see this word?	

Building Vocabulary: Predictions

How do you predict these words will be used in "A Profile in Courage" and "The New Deal"? Write your answers in the second column. Next, read the selections. Then, clarify your answers in the third column.

Word	My prediction for how the word will be used	How the word is actually used
sheltered		
public service		
vaccination		
charities		
foreclosure		
traitor		

Writing: Character Map

Use what you have learned about Franklin Delano Roosevelt's accomplishments to fill in the character map.

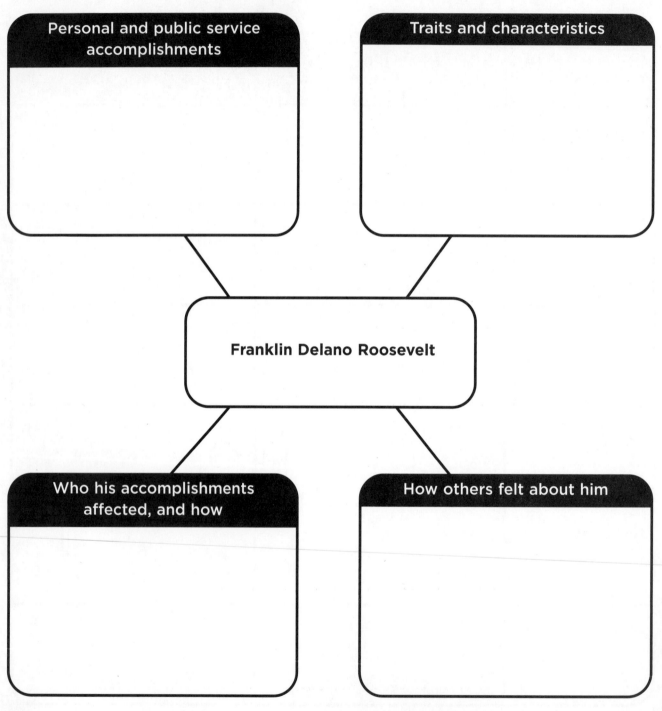

Personal and public service accomplishments

Traits and characteristics

Franklin Delano Roosevelt

Who his accomplishments affected, and how

How others felt about him

Writing: Biographical Sketch

Use the character map you completed on page 140 to write a
biographical sketch of Franklin Delano Roosevelt.

_____

_____

_____

_____

_____

_____

_____

_____

_____

_____

_____

_____

_____

_____

_____

_____

_____

_____

_____

_____

_____

_____

_____

Building Vocabulary: Creating a Word Web

From the word box below, choose a word or phrase that's familiar to you and write it in the center oval. Write other words around the oval that help define the word or that you associate with it. Then write the complete definition at the bottom of the page.

sheltered   public service   vaccination   foreclosure   traitor

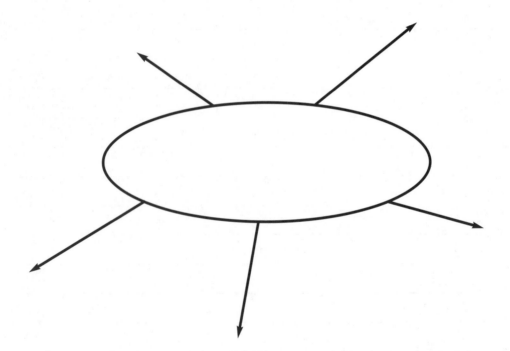

Write the complete definition here:

Building Vocabulary: Using a Word Map

Choose a vocabulary word and write it in the center box. Then fill in as much of the word map as you can. After you read "What a Collection!" complete the word map and make any necessary corrections.

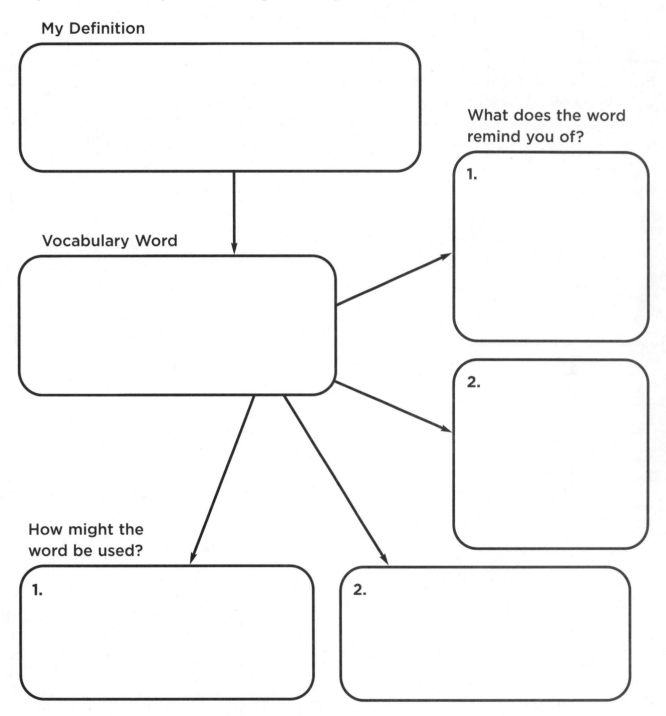

My Definition

What does the word remind you of?

1.

2.

Vocabulary Word

How might the word be used?

1.

2.

Writing: Retelling

Read the three sentences below from page 41 of the selection. Retell them in your own words. Remember that your retelling should have the same meaning as the original sentences. If you are unsure what the original sentences mean, discuss them with a partner before retelling them.

The bottle bug bit Rick when he was sixteen years old. Since then, he's discovered antique bottles on riverbanks, along construction sites, and in old trash deposits tucked away in the woods. He cautions his son to look for rusty metal and broken glass, telltale signs of old trash heaps buried by time.

My Retelling:

_____

_____

_____

_____

_____

_____

_____

_____

_____

_____

_____

_____

_____

_____

_____

_____

Building Vocabulary: Related Words

Choose a word from the box or another word from the selection and write it in the first column. Next, write a related word in the second column. Then, write the definition of each related word.

| collectibles | curator | difference | donations |
| examine | handling | obsession | |

	Selected Word	Related Word	Definition
1.			
2.			
3.			

Building Vocabulary: Related Words Puzzle

The words in the first column are from all the selections you have read
in this magazine so far. Find a word related to the word in the first
column to complete each sentence. Then use that related word to fill
in the puzzle below. The first one has been done for you.

Word	Related Word
1. vaccination ↓	The nurse prepared to give the flu ___vaccine___ .
2. circulation →	I started my picture of the clock by drawing a _____ .
3. composition →	The musician _____ the song in honor of her mother.
4. occupation ↓	The new toy kept my brother _____ for a while, but then he grew bored.
5. decimated ↓	Moving the _____ point to the left by just one place makes a number ten times larger!
6. memento →	The principal wrote a _____ to teachers reminding them that next Thursday was the last day to turn in grades.

Building Vocabulary: Knowledge Rating Chart

Show your knowledge of each word by adding as much information
as you can to the other boxes in the row.

Word	Define or Use in a Sentence	Where Have I Seen or Heard It?	How Is It Used in the Selection?	Looks Like (Words or Sketch)
biodiversity				
submersible				
palette				
polyps				
endemic				
unpredictability				

Writing: Notes for Visualizing

Which sleeping accommodation on the bottom of page 50 could you visualize the best? Describe it below. Include as many details as you can. Then draw a picture to show what you "saw in your mind."

The sleeping accommodation I could visualize best was _____

_____

_____

Some details I "saw in my mind" include _____

_____

_____

_____

Now draw what you visualized.

© Great Source. Copying is permitted; see page ii.

Building Vocabulary: Using Context to Understand a Word

Select a word from the box or another word from the selection that you defined from the context. Then complete the statements and answer the questions about your word.

biodiversity   palette   polyps   endemic   unpredictability

My Word in Context:

I think this word means _____

because _____

_____

_____

My word is _____

_____

My word is not _____

_____

Where else might I find this word? _____

_____

_____

What makes this an important word to know? _____

_____

_____

_____

Building Vocabulary: Knowledge Rating Chart

Show your knowledge of each word by adding information to the other boxes in the row.

Word	Define or Use in a Sentence	Where Have I Seen or Heard It?	How Is It Used in the Selection?	Looks Like (Words or Sketch)
extravaganza				
incredulously				
philosophical				
devastated				
depression				

Writing: Character Map

Use what you have learned about Jasper to fill in the character map.

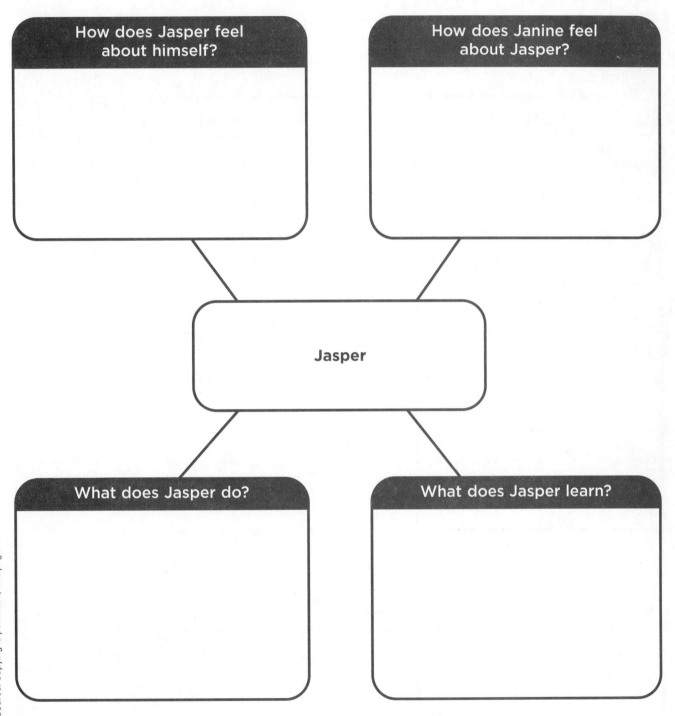

How does Jasper feel
about himself?

How does Janine feel
about Jasper?

Jasper

What does Jasper do?

What does Jasper learn?

Building Vocabulary: Word Roots

Write words in the first column that contain the Latin root *cred*. Write a definition for each word. Use a dictionary to help you, if you wish.

cred means "to believe"

Word	Definition
incredulously	said or done in a way that shows disbelief

Money • Jasper Norton Wants to Know: Can Money Buy Love?

Building Vocabulary: Making Associations

Pick two words from the box below. Think about what you already know about each word and answer the questions.

| retail | sweatshops | enduring | abrasion |

Word _____

What do you think about when you read this word? _____

_____

Who might use this word? _____

_____

What do you already know about this word? _____

_____

Word _____

What do you think about when you read this word? _____

_____

Who might use this word? _____

_____

What do you already know about this word? _____

_____

Now watch for these words in the selection. Were you on the right track?

Writing: Double-entry Journal

In the first column, write phrases or sentences from "The Real Cost of
Jeans" that were meaningful to you. In the second column, explain why.

Quotation	Why It Is Meaningful

Writing: Letter

Use your notes from page 154 to write a letter to the president of your favorite jeans company.

_____ ,

Building Vocabulary: Compound Words

Look through the selection "The Real Cost of Jeans" to find as many compound words as you can. Write each compound word in the first column. Then, write the two words that form the compound. Finally, write a definition of the word.

Compound Word	Word 1	Word 2	Definition of Compound Word
anything	any	thing	any object

The Reading Process

The Reading Process has three parts: Before Reading, During Reading, and After Reading.

BEFORE Reading

Preview the Material

Look over the selection before you read. Does the selection look like a short story or other fiction? If so, look at the title, introduction, or illustrations. Does the selection look like nonfiction? If so, look for headings, boldfaced words, photos, or captions. Also, ask yourself how the information is organized. Is the author comparing or contrasting information about the topic? Is the information presented in a sequence using signal words like *first, second, third,* or *finally?* Understanding how the author is presenting information will help you to recognize key information as you read.

Make Predictions

When you make predictions, you actively connect with the words on the page. Think about what you know already about the subject or anything you see. Then, think of yourself as a text detective, putting together what you know with new details in the text. Predict what you think will happen, why an event caused something to happen, or what might come next in a series of events. Then, double-check what you have read to confirm or support your predictions. Did your prediction match the text? If not, use what you have learned to revise your prediction, and keep on reading.

Set a Purpose

Begin by reviewing what you already know about the topic or situation in the text. Then, think about what you want to find out.

> ### *Questions to Ask Yourself Before Reading:*
>
> - Before I read this material, what do I think it is going to be about?
> - After looking through the article, what do I already know about this subject?
> - What should I be thinking about as I read?

Engage with the Text

As your eyes look at the words, your brain should be working to make connections between the words and what you already know. Have you had a similar experience as one of the characters in a story you are reading? Do you know someone like the character? Have you read another book about the topic? You will also want to connect what you read to the predictions you made before reading. Confirm, revise, and predict again is a cycle that continues until the reading material is completed. All of these questions will go on inside your head. Sometimes, though, it helps to think out loud or write.

Monitor Your Understanding

As you read, stop from time to time and ask yourself, "Do I understand what I just read?" If the text doesn't make sense, there are several steps that you can take.

- Go back and reread the text carefully.
- Read on to see if more information helps you understand.
- Pull together the author's ideas in a summary.
- Retell, or say in your own words, the events that have happened.
- Picture in your mind what the author described.
- Look for context clues or word-structure clues to help you figure out hard words.

This takes some practice. Remember, to be a successful reader, you are an active reader. Make an effort to check your understanding every so often when you read a new selection.

> ### Questions to Ask Yourself
> ### During *Reading:*
>
> - As I am reading, what important details am I finding?
> - Which of these ideas seem to be the most important?
> - Does this information fit with anything I already know?
> - What do I see in my mind as I read this material?
> - Do I understand the information in the charts or tables? Does it help me to understand what I am reading?

Summarize

Reread to locate the most important ideas in the story or article.

Respond and Reflect

Talk with a partner about what you have read. What did you learn from the text? What questions do you have? Talking about reading helps you understand better what you have read.

Ask Questions

Try asking yourself questions that begin like this:

Can I compare or contrast? . . . evaluate?   . . . connect?   . . . examine?
. . . analyze?   . . . relate?

Engage with the Text

Good readers engage with the text all the time, even when they have finished reading. When you tie events in your life or something else you have read to what you are currently reading, you become more involved with your reading. In the process, you are learning more about your values, relationships in your family, and problems in the world around you.

> ### Questions to Ask Yourself After Reading:
>
> - Have I learned something that makes me want to change the way I think about this topic?
>
> - What was this article about?
>
> - Are there parts of this material that I really want to remember?
>
> - What was the author trying to tell me?

Glossary

A

abominable (a BOM i nih bul) *adjective.* detestable; loathsome

abrasion (a BRA zhun) *noun.* the process of wearing down by rubbing or scraping

accurate (AK yer it) *adjective.* without error; correct

adhesive (ad HEE siv) *noun.* a substance that provides stickiness, like paste or cement

alterations (al ter RAY shuns) *noun.* changes from the original

alternative (al TERN a tiv) *adjective.* a choice of two or more possibilities; not the usual or conventional

altruistic (al tru IS tik) *adjective.* a person or behavior that shows unselfish concern for others

analyze (AN uhl iyz) *verb.* to examine carefully by breaking into parts

anthropologist an thro POL i jist) *noun.* a scientist who studies the origins of humans

antimicrobial (an ty my KRO be al) *adjective.* capable of killing or slowing the growth of microorganisms, such as bacteria

aqueducts (AK wi ductz) *noun.* passageways designed to carry water

archaeologists (ar key OL o jists) *noun.* scientists who study past human life and culture by examining physical evidence, such as buildings and tools

artifacts (AR ti fakts) *noun.* objects made by humans that are of historical interest

aspiring (as PYR ing) *verb.* reaching toward a great goal

assimilate (a SIM i layt) *verb.* to make similar and absorb

asteroid belt (AS teh royd belt) *noun.* the part of the solar system between Jupiter and Mars that contains most of the system's asteroids, or small orbiting bodies

astronomer (a STRON e mer) *noun.* a scientist who studies the stars, planets, and other bodies in outer space

atoms (AT oms) *noun.* the smallest part of all matter

B

barbs (barbs) *noun.* sharp points projecting in the opposite direction of the main point of weapons or tools

baroque (buh ROKE) *adjective.* of, or similar to, the extremely ornate style of art and music popular in Europe from approximately 1600 to 1750

bilingual (by LIHNG gwal) *adjective.* able to use two languages

biodiversity (by oh dih VERS i tee) *noun.* the number and variety of living things

bizarre (bi ZAR) *adjective.* extremely odd or strange

bristled (BRIS uhld) *verb.* to react in an annoyed manner

Buddhist (BOOD ist) *noun.* a believer in the teachings of Buddha, an Indian mystic who lived approximately 2500 years ago

C

canteen (kan TEEN) *noun.* a water bottle used by soldiers or travelers to carry water

cask (kask) *noun.* a barrel used to hold liquid

cathedral (kuh THEE drul) *noun.* a large and important church

census (SEN suss) *noun.* an official count of the number of people living in an area, state, or country

characteristics (care uk tuh RISS tiks) *noun.* traits or aspects that make a particular person or thing distinctive

charisma (kuh RIZZ muh) *noun.* personal magnetism or charm that attracts others and makes them easier to influence or excite

charitable (CHAIR it uh bul) *adjective.* generous, prone to giving

charities (CHAIR it tees) *noun.* organizations that help the needy

charting (CHAR ting) *verb.* creating a plan for how to do or achieve something; plotting a course of direction to travel

circulation (sir kyuh LAY shun) *noun.* the movement of blood through the body; the number of people who read a magazine or newspaper

civilians (sih VIL yens) *noun.* persons who are not in the military

collectibles (kuh LECT ih buls) *noun.* items considered valuable or interesting enough to collect or acquire many of them, such as coins or baseball cards

commemorated (kuh MEM uh ray ted) *verb.* to have honored the memory of something with a ceremony, holiday, or specially created object

commission (kuh MISH un) *verb.* to hire someone to do a project or create a particular object or work of art

components (kum POH nents) *noun.* parts, as in the individual pieces or elements that create the whole

composition (kom puh ZIH shun) *noun.* what something is made of, as in the ingredients, elements, or substances that it is composed of; in the arts, a musical work or an essay

confidential (kon fih DEN shul) *adjective.* secret, as in information shared only with a few people

confiscated (KON fih skay ted) *adjective.* to have been taken away by a person with authority

confrontations (kon frun TAY shuns) *noun.* hostile arguments, fights, or battles

congestion (kon JEST shun) *noun.* overcrowding, as in roads with too much traffic

continuity (kon tuh NU ih tee) *noun.* the state of being uninterrupted, as in remaining the same over time

controversies (KON truh vur sees) *noun.* public issues that cause heated arguments because people hold strongly opposed opinions

correspondence (kar uh SPON dens) *noun.* written communication such as letters or e-mail

cosmos (KAHZ mohs) *noun.* everything that exists on Earth and in the whole universe

counterparts (KOWN ter parts) *noun.* a person or thing that has a role or function similar to another but in a different situation.

crater (KRAY ter) *noun.* a large, bowl-shaped hole in the ground caused by the impact of a meteor or a bomb

crinoid (krih NOYD) *noun.* sea creatures that do not have backbones but that do have cup-shaped bodies and multiple feathery arms that surround a mouth at their center

cumbersome (KUM ber sum) *adjective.* difficult to handle, carry, or hold due to an awkward shape or heavy weight

curator (KYUR ay ter) *noun.* a person who decides what will be shown in an art exhibit or museum

D

decide (duh SIYD) *verb.* to choose, to select, to make up one's mind

data (DAH tuh) *noun.* facts, figures, or information that are collected to better understand something

debris (duh BREE) *noun.* rubble or wreckage

decimated (DESS uh MAYT ted) *verb.* to have caused extreme damage and destruction to something

deduction (DEE duk shun) *noun.* a conclusion reached by considering known facts

degrading (dee GRAYD ing) *adjective.* something that dishonors, disgraces, or humiliates

depicted (dee PIKT ed) *verb.* to have described something in writing or to have represented something or someone with an artwork, such as a drawing or sculpture

depression (duh PREH shun) *noun.* a sunken area that is lower than the surrounding area on the surface of something; an illness that causes one to feel sad

destination (dess tuh NAY shun) *noun.* the place one travels to on a trip, or aims to reach

devastated (DEV uh stay ted) *adjective.* completely destroyed or ruined; terribly upset and shocked by something

devastating (DEV uh stayt ing) *adjective.* causing complete destruction; causing extreme upset or shock

devastation (dev uh STAY shun) *noun.* total destruction, the state of being completely wrecked and ruined; ALSO the feeling of total upset and shock

dialects (DYE uh lekts) *noun.* varieties of a language, spoken by a group of people in a distinct area

dilemmas (dih LEM uhs) *noun.* difficult situations in which both options for action will have similar and often negative outcomes

disability (diss uh BIL ih tee) *noun.* something that hinders or impairs

dismay (diss MAY) *noun.* a feeling of disappointment

displaced (dis PLAYSD) *adjective.* removed from the normal location, especially to have forced people to leave their home or countries and live elsewhere

dock (dok) *noun.* a landing area on the shore where ships load and unload

documentary (dok yuh MEM tuh ree) *noun.* a film that present the facts of a subject through interviews, real-life film footage, and narration

domain (doh MAYN) *noun.* the area that a person in power rules over or governs; an area of study, activity, or interest

drastically (DRASS tik lee) *adverb.* extremely or severely, as in taking radical action

dubious (DOO bee us) *adjective.* doubtful, as in something that seems suspicious or not right

dwindling (DWIND ling) *verb.* to decrease in amount slowly until almost nothing is left

E

ecosystem (EE koh sis tem) *noun.* all the living things in an area, and the environment in which they live

emancipation (ee man suh PAY shun) *noun.* the freeing of someone from the control of another often while also granting them equal rights

empathize (EM puh thize) *verb.* to understand, share, or be sensitive to the feelings or situation of another

encroaching (en KROHCH ing) *verb.* advancing beyond the existing limit or border

endemic (en DEM ik) *adjective.* found mainly or only in a particular area or group of people

enduring (en DUR ing) *adjective.* lasting

entrepreneurs (on truh pruh NORES) *noun.* people who start businesses

espionage (ESS pee uh nazh) *noun.* spying to obtain secret information

exclusion (ek SKLOO zhun) *noun.* not allowing someone to participate or not considering something to be part of a group

exile (ek ZILE) *verb.* to banish, to force someone to leave their country

exodus (ek ZUH duss) *noun.* when a large number of people leave an area or a country all at once

extravaganza (ek strav uh GANZ uh) *noun.* a big and impressive event or performance

F

facilitated (fuh SIL uh tay ted) *verb.* to have assisted or helped something to happen

facilities (fuh SIL ih tees) *noun.* buildings designed to be used for a specific purpose

fashion (FASH un) *noun.* the current trend or style, such as clothing that is popular; *verb.* to attach, combine, or build

flock (flok) *noun.* a group of birds that live together; *verb.* large numbers of people being drawn to something

foreclosed (for KLOSED) *adjective.* seized property that has been taken away by the bank because the owner did not pay the loan on it

foreclosure (for KLOZH or) *noun.* the act of a bank taking away property because the loan on it has not been paid

forensic (fah REN zik) *adjective.* scientifically researched evidence or information used in a court of law

fraternal (fra TER nul) *adjective.* when twins are born from separate eggs as opposed to identical twins, which are born from one egg

fulfill (ful FIL) *verb.* to carry out a task or do all that is expected

G

gauge (gayj) *verb.* to determine an amount

gawkers (GOK urs) *noun.* people who stare at something; onlookers

genetic (jeh NEH tik) *adjective.* related to physical characteristics that people inherit

genus (GEE nus) *noun.* a class, or particular kind, of living things

gravity (GRAV eh tee) *noun.* the force that makes things fall to the ground

guarantees (gar un TEES) *noun.* promises that something will be done

H

habitat (HAB ih tat) *noun.* the place where a person, plant, or animal lives

haphazardly (hap HAZ urd lee) *adverb.* happening in a way that hasn't been planned

hiatus (hy AY tus) *noun.* an unexpected gap or interruption in time

hominids (HOM uh nidz) *noun.* any member of the family of two-legged primates, including humans and their ancestors

hull (hul) *noun.* the main body of a ship

I

impact (IM pakt) *noun.* the strong effect of one thing on another

implement (IM pluh ment) *verb.* to carry something out; to put a plan into action

impressions (im PRESH unz) *noun.* marks made by something hard having been pressed onto a softer surface

incredulously (in KRED juh luss lee) *adverb.* showing disbelief

indentured servant (in DEN churd SUR vent) *noun.* a person who works for another for an agreed upon period of time

inducted (in DUK tid) *verb.* to be formally placed as a member in a position or office

infinitely (IN fih nit lee) *adverb.* having no limits or boundaries

infrared light (in fruh RED lite) *noun.* specific invisible wavelengths of radiation

infrasound (IN fruh sownd) *noun.* sounds too low for the human ear to hear

internees (in tur NEEZ) *noun.* people who are forced to live in a prison-like space in wartime

internment (in TURN ment) *noun.* the period of time in which internees are kept in a prison-like space in wartime

interpretations (in tur prih TAY shunz) *noun.* explanations that help people know the meaning of something

interpreter (in TUR prih tur) *noun.* a person who translates one language into another to help foreign-language speakers communicate

invertebrates (in VUR tuh brates) *noun.* animals without a backbone or spinal column

J

jam session (jam SESH un) *noun.* a period of time that is spent making new music or practicing new musical techniques

K

kiosk (KEE osk) *noun.* a booth used as a newsstand or a place to sell things

knock-offs (NOK offs) *noun.* imitations of a distinctive product

L

landscape architect (land scayp ARE kih tekt) *noun.* a professional who plans and designs outdoor spaces such as gardens, parks, and building grounds

larva (LAR vuh) *noun.* the earliest, wormlike, wingless stage of life for an insect before it becomes an adult insect

larvae (LAR vay) *noun.* more than one larva

larynx (LAIR inx) *noun.* the chamber in the throat that contains the vocal chords, also known as the voice box

latent (LAYT int) *adjective.* something that exists but that is not yet active or apparent

legislation (ledj ih SLAY shun) *noun.* laws made by a body of government such as the U.S. Congress

liberation (lib ah RAY shun) *noun.* the act of being freed from oppression or slavery

luminous (LOO muh nus) *adjective.* something bright that gives off a lot of light

lush (lush) *adjective.* growing thickly and densely as in thriving plants

M

mandatory (MAN duh tor ee) *adjective.* required

manicured (MAN ih cyurd) *adjective.* neatly trimmed and shaped

manuals (MAN yoo uhls) *noun.* small books that provide instruction on how to use something or do something

mariachi (mah ree ATCH ee) *noun.* a Mexican street musician or a group of such musicians

meager (MEE gur) *adjective.* small in amount

memento (muh MEN tow) *noun.* a keepsake or souvenir that reminds of the past

menacing (MEN us ing) *adjective.* scary or seemingly dangerous

merchandise (MER chan dys) *noun.* products bought and sold at a business or store

migrant labor (MY grent LAY bur) *noun.* workers that travel from farm to farm to pick crops as soon as they ripen

migration (MY gray shun) *noun.* people leaving their home country to live in a new country; birds or animals traveling to other regions to breed or avoid cold weather

mimic (MIM ik) *verb.* to copy or imitate the behavior or actions of another

minted (MIN ted) *adjective.* pressed or stamped from metal

mnemonic (nih MON ick) *adjective.* assisting the memory

modified (MOD uh fyde) *adjective.* changed or altered

module (MODGE ool) *noun.* a self-contained unit, such as a specific area of a spacecraft

moor (more) *noun.* a high area of open land

molecules (MALL uh kyuls) *noun.* the smallest particle of a substance that still has two or more atoms

mournful (MORN ful) *adjective.* sad or sorrowful

N

nanoscience (NAN oh sy uns) *noun.* the science of building electrical devices out of individual atoms or molecules

nauseated (NAW zee ay ted) *adjective.* feeling sick in the stomach

nectar (NEK ter) *noun.* the liquid found in flowers that insects and hummingbirds eat; the food or drink of the Greek and Roman gods

negotiate (nih GO shee ayt) *verb.* to discuss, bargain, or deal with another to come to an agreement

nurture (NER chur) *verb.* to feed or help grow and develop

O

oblivious (uh BLIV ee us) *adjective.* completely unaware, uninformed of, or ignorant

obsequious (ub SEE kwee us) *adjective.* behaving like a servant or slave, overly eager to serve and obey

observatory (ub ZURV uh tor ee) *noun.* a scientific building that houses a telescope used to observe stars, planets, comets and other space phenomena

obsessed (ub SEST) *adjective.* to have one's thoughts completely occupied by one thing or one emotion

obsession (ub SEH shun) *noun.* an object or idea that completely occupies one's thoughts

occupation (ok yuh PAY shun) *noun.* job or profession

oral history (OR ul HISS tor ee) *noun.* historical information gathered through interviews, videotaping, or tape recording

orbiting (OR bit ing) *adverb.* a planet, moon, satellite or other object in space that is circling around another object

ornate (or NAYT) *adjective.* decorated with a lot of detail

ossified (OS uh fyd) *adjective.* changed into bone

P

paleontologist (pay lee on TALL oh gist) *noun.* a scientist who studies life in the past by examining fossils

palette (PAL it) *noun.* the range of colors used by an artist

parching (PARCH ing) *verb.* becoming very dry

patent (PAT int) *noun.* a legal right to make or sell an invention

permits (PUR mits) *noun.* documents giving permission to do something

perpetrator (PUR peh tray tor) *noun.* person responsible for committing a crime

pertain (pur TAYN) *verb.* to relate to

philanthropies (fih LAN thro peez) *noun.* charitable organizations

philosophical (fil uh SAHF ih kul) *adjective.* relating to beliefs about the meaning of life and how to live one's life

plaza (PLAH zuh) *noun.* a public square in a city or town

pollen (PAHL in) *noun.* fine grains produced by seed plants

pollinate (PAHL in ayt) *verb.* to spread pollen to plants so that they can reproduce

polyps (PAHL ips) *noun.* small tube-shaped water animals

portable (POR tuh bul) *adjective.* can be carried or moved easily

predators (PRED uh tors) *noun.* animals that kill and eat other animals

prefix (PREE fix) *noun.* a letter or group of letters attached to the beginning of a word that changes the meaning of the word

prominent (PROM ih nent) *adjective.* describes a person who is well known and important

promotion (pro MO shun) *noun.* encouraging the popularity or sale of something; advertising

propel (pro PEL) *verb.* to cause to move forward, often with force

prototypes (PRO toe types) *noun.* working models of something

protruded (pro TRU ded) *verb.* stuck out

provenance (PRAHV eh nents) *noun.* proof of authenticity or past ownership

public service (pub lik SERV iss) *noun.* working for the government to help the general public

pygmy (PIG me) *noun.* an unusually small animal, bird, or human

R

reef (reef) *noun.* a line of rocks, sand, or coral just under the surface of the water

refugees (REF u gees) *noun.* people who flee to a safe place in times of war

regimented (REJ uh ment ed) *verb.* strictly organized

renounced (re NOUNST) *verb.* gave up in a formal way

replicate (REP lih kate) *verb.* to copy or reproduce

reposition (ree po ZISH un) *verb.* to put in a new position

reputation (rep u TAY shun) *noun.* the respect and admiration a person has

reservoir (REZ er vwar) *noun.* a natural or artificial pond or lake where water is stored

resume (reh ZOOM) *verb.* to begin again

retail (REE tail) *adjective.* engaged in the sale of goods directly to consumers

rhythmic (RITH mik) *adjective.* a sound with a regular movement or beat

ruckus (RUK us) *noun.* a noisy disturbance

rugby (RUG bee) *noun.* a sport similar to American football

S

safe house (sayf hous) *noun.* a house or apartment used as a hiding place

salvage (SAL vij) *verb.* to save goods, especially from a sunken ship

satyr (SAY ter) *noun.* a mythological figure that is half man and half goat

scripts (skripts) *noun.* texts of plays

scuba (SKOO buh) *noun.* portable device for breathing underwater

sediment (SED eh ment) *noun.* material that settles to the bottom of a liquid

seethe (seethe) *verb.* to be very excited or agitated

sentinels (SEN teh nehls) *noun.* guards

sharecroppers (SHARE krop urs) *noun.* tenant farmers who give part of their crops to the landlord as rent

sheltered (SHEL terd) *verb.* covered or protected

shortchange (short chaynj) *verb.* to treat unfairly

sign language (sine LANG widg) *noun.* a language that uses hand movements as a means of communication

skeptical (SKEP tih kul) *adjective.* given to doubt; questioning

smug (smug) *adjective.* feeling very satisfied with oneself

sophisticated (so FIS tih kayt id) *adjective.* very complex or complicated

specialize (SPESH uh lize) *verb.* to concentrate on a particular activity or field of study

species (SPEE sheez) *noun.* a basic biological category of related animals or plants

spirituals (SPEER ih choo ulz) *noun.* religious folk songs of African American origin

sprawl (sprawl) *noun.* an extension outward

static (STAT ik) *adjective.* having no movement

statistics (stuh TISS ticks) *noun.* facts based on the study of numbers

stereotypes (STARE e oh types) *noun.* fixed ideas about people that are often incorrect

stipend (STY pend) *noun.* a fixed and regular payment, such as a salary or allowance

submersible (sub MER seh bul) *noun.* a vessel that can operate underwater

subterranean (sub teh RAY nee an) *adjective.* beneath the earth's surface; underground

superstition (soo per STISH un) *noun.* a belief not based on human reason or scientific knowledge

surrogate (SUR ih get) *noun.* a substitute

surveyed (SIR vayd) *verb.* measured an area of land

sweatshops (SWET shops) *noun.* factories where employees work long hours in poor conditions for low wages

T

terminology (tur meh NOL eh jee) *noun.* the vocabulary of terms used in a particular field

tether (TETH er) *noun.* a rope, chain, or other device for holding something in place

thwart (thwort) *verb.* to stop someone from doing something

tirade (TIE rayd) *noun.* a long angry or violent speech

tolerance (TAHL ur ens) *noun.* respecting the beliefs and practices of others

tracts (trax) *noun.* short pieces of writing intended to influence the opinions of others

traitor (TRAY tor) *noun.* one who betrays one's country

translators (TRANS lay tors) *noun.* people who change words into a different language; interpreters

transmissions (trans MISH ens) *noun.* messages broadcast from one place to another

treaties (TREE tees) *noun.* formal agreements between two or more countries

tribulations (trib u LAY shunz) *noun.* problems that cause great distress or suffering

tsunamis (soo NAH mees) *noun.* very large ocean waves caused by underwater earthquakes

U

under-utilized (un dur YOOT ih lized) *adjective.* not used as much as possible

unpredictability (un pre dikt uh BIL uh tee) *adverb.* tendency to change suddenly and without reason

V

vaccination (vak suh NAY shun) *noun.* an inoculation that protects against a particular disease

vacuum (VAK yoom) *noun.* a state of emptiness; a void

velocity (veh LOS ih tee) *noun.* rate of speed

vendors (VEN durs) *noun.* people who sell goods

vestiges (VES tih jez) *noun.* traces or remains of something that once existed

vivid (VIV id) *adjective.* bright and distinct

W

wane (wayn) *verb.* to gradually get smaller in size or intensity

warped (worpt) *adjective.* strange and sometimes unpleasant

Personal Word Bank

Words	Definitions

Personal Word Bank

Words	Definitions

Personal Word Bank

Words	Definitions

Personal Word Bank

Words	Definitions

Personal Word Bank

Words	Definitions